DATE DUE

HOW OUR BLOOD CIRCULATES

Text: Mercè Parramón
Illustrations: Marcel Socías

Cómo Circula Nuestra Sangre © Copyright Parramón
Ediciones, S.A., Published by Parramón Ediciones, S.A.,
Barcelona, Spain.

How Our Blood Circulates copyright © 1994 by Chelsea
House Publishers, a subsidiary of Haights Cross
Communications.
All rights reserved

© 2001 by Chelsea House Publishers, a subsidiary of
Haights Cross Communications.

Printed and bound in Spain.

Chelsea House Publishers
1974 Sproul Road, Suite 400
Broomall, PA 19008-0914

The Chelsea House world wide web address is
www.chelseahouse.com

Library of Congress Cataloging-in-Publication Data
Applied for

ISBN 0-7910-2127-0

Contents

The Circulatory System	4
The Composition of Blood	6
Red Blood Cells	8
White Blood Cells	10
Clotting	12
The Heart	14
How the Heart Beats	16
Circulating Oxygen	18
Systemic Circulation	20
Blood Vessels	22
The Lymph System	24
Lymph Vessels	26
Simple Experiments	28
Glossary	30
Index	31

INVISIBLE WORLD

HOW OUR BLOOD CIRCULATES

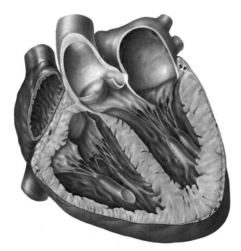

CHELSEA HOUSE PUBLISHERS

Philadelphia

The Circulatory System

The survival of the human body depends on a steady supply of food and oxygen reaching all of its cells. Meanwhile, carbon dioxide and other waste materials produced by the cells must be removed. The circulatory system transports these materials throughout the body.

The materials are carried in a fluid known as blood, which travels through a complex system of tubes called blood vessels. There are three main types of blood vessels—arteries, veins, and capillaries—and blood is pumped through them by a mass of muscles known as the heart.

Blood picks up a fresh supply of oxygen in the lungs before it is pumped to every cell. The oxygen-poor blood then returns to the heart and is pumped to the lungs for more oxygen.

Blood also picks up other important substances, such as nutrients from the digestive system and hormones from the glands, and carries them to parts of the body where they are needed. At the same time, the blood picks up waste products and carries them to the kidneys, lungs, and skin, which help expel them from the body.

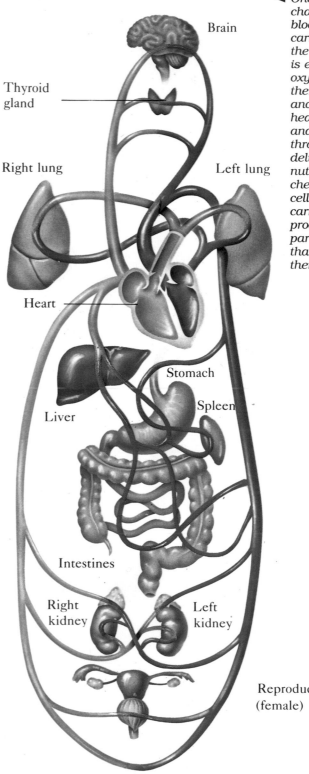

Brain

Thyroid gland

Right lung

Left lung

Heart

Stomach

Spleen

Liver

Intestines

Right kidney

Left kidney

Reproductive organs (female)

◄ *One of the heart's chambers pumps blood containing carbon dioxide to the lungs, where it is exchanged for oxygen. The blood then flows back to another of the heart's chambers, and it is pumped through the body, delivering oxygen, nutrients, and chemicals to the cells. The blood also carries waste products to the parts of the body that will get rid of them.*

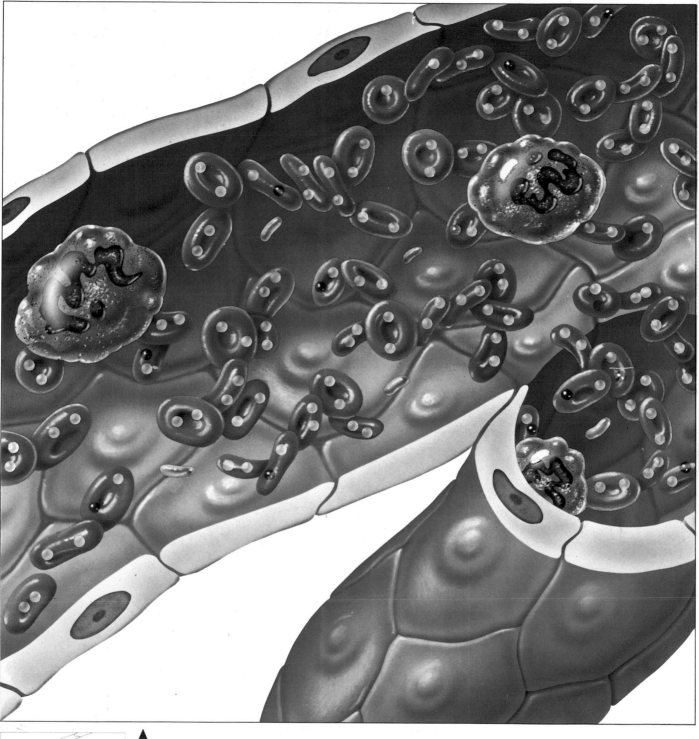

A view inside a capillary, showing the main components of the blood (numbered in the inset). The red blood cells **(1)** transport oxygen and carbon dioxide. The white blood cells **(2)** are part of the body's defense system. The platelets **(3)** help the blood form a clot after an injury. The capillary walls **(4)** are made up of a single layer of cells.

The Composition of Blood

Our blood consists of several types of cells carried around in a yellow liquid called blood plasma. Water makes up about 90 percent of plasma, which contains nutrients, proteins, hormones, and waste products in addition to the blood cells.

There are three types of blood cells: red blood cells (erythrocytes), white blood cells (leucocytes), and platelets (thrombocytes). Red and white blood cells are also known as corpuscles.

Red blood cells look like flattened, doughnut-shaped discs. There are 5.5 million in every .4 cubic inch of blood (about the size of a pinhead). They contain a compound called hemoglobin, which is rich in iron. Hemoglobin picks up oxygen in the lungs, which turns the hemoglobin bright red. As the blood goes through the body, the hemoglobin delivers the oxygen to the cells in exchange for the waste product carbon dioxide.

White blood cells are much bigger than red blood cells. There are between 4,000 and 10,000 in every .4 cubic inch of blood. Unlike red blood cells, white blood cells have a nucleus. Most white blood cells can move around in the bloodstream, which enables them to play an important part in the body's defense system. They go into action in whatever part of the body they are needed.

There are several types of white blood cells. Lymphocytes, made in the lymph tissue, form antibodies to attack any foreign substances that enter the body. Monocytes, made in the bone marrow, swallow up foreign bodies.

Blood platelets are oval-shaped cells made in the bone marrow. There are around 250,000 to 500,000 platelets in every .4 cubic inch of blood. They take part in the clotting process: when a blood vessel breaks, platelets cluster around the broken blood vessel and help seal it.

When something sharp, such as a splinter, enters the body (1), platelets (2) help to seal the wound. Microbes (3) that enter with the splinter will be dealt with by white blood cells (4). Red blood cells (5) carry oxygen or carbon dioxide around the body. All blood cells float in a liquid called plasma. ▼

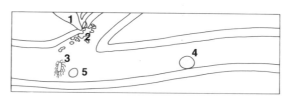

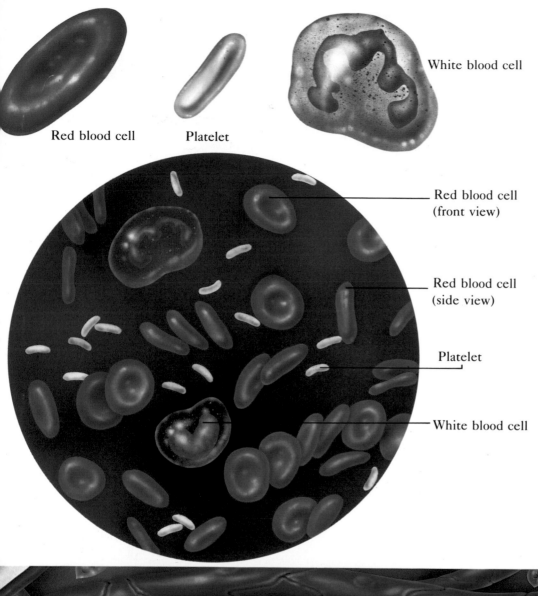

Red blood cell

Platelet

White blood cell

Red blood cell
(front view)

Red blood cell
(side view)

Platelet

White blood cell

◄

*Blood cells as seen
through a
microscope.*

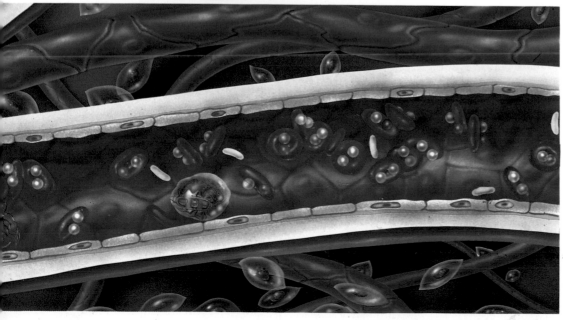

Red Blood Cells

Red blood cells, which are formed in the bone marrow, make up about 45 percent of the blood. About 200,000 billion are produced each day, and they have an average life of 120 days. As they grow older, they become fragile and lose their shape. They also shrink to about a third of their original size.

The red blood cells eventually break up into smaller particles in the liver and the spleen. Most of the old red blood cells are surrounded and destroyed in the spleen. Any cells not destroyed in the spleen are finished off in the liver. The liver then stores the iron from the hemoglobin, until the blood carries it to the red marrow in the bones and uses it to make new red blood cells.

The body's supply of red blood cells is completely renewed every four months.

▲
The side and front views of a red blood cell. It contains the red compound hemoglobin, which can combine with oxygen and carbon dioxide.

A hemoglobin molecule. The four red disks are heme molecules, and the long globin strands are amino acids.

▼

Heme molecules   Amino acids

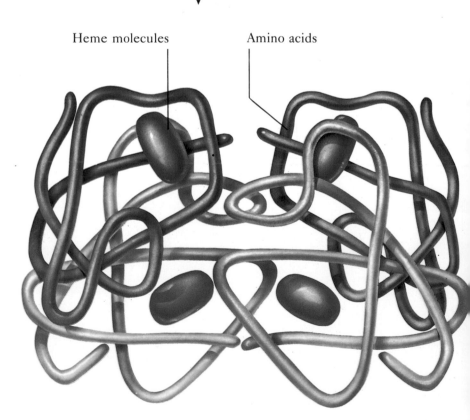

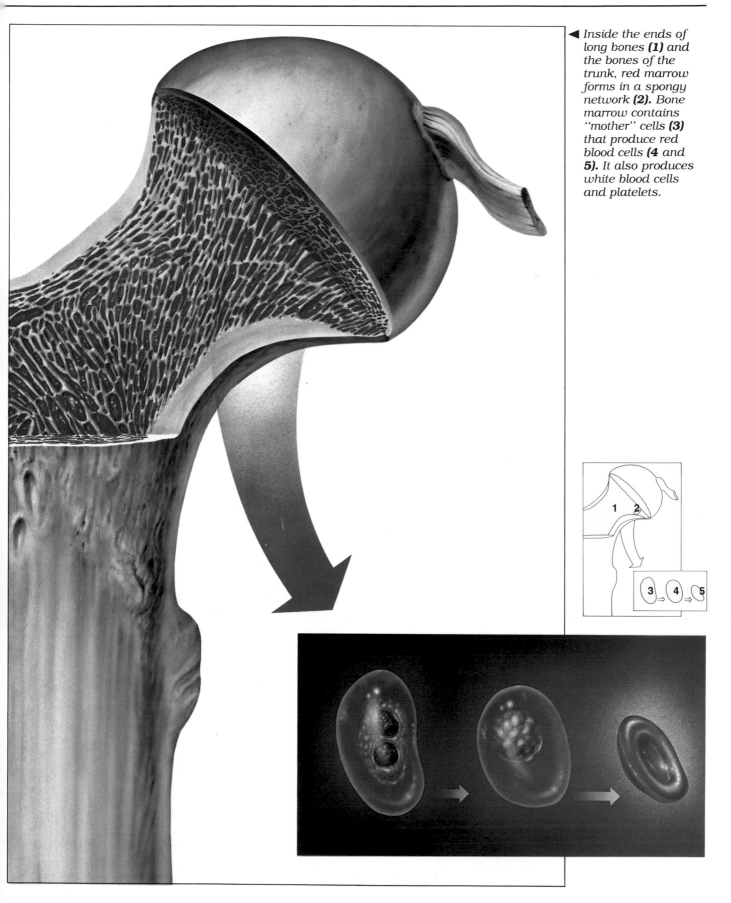

◀ Inside the ends of long bones **(1)** and the bones of the trunk, red marrow forms in a spongy network **(2).** Bone marrow contains "mother" cells **(3)** that produce red blood cells **(4** and **5).** It also produces white blood cells and platelets.

White Blood Cells

White blood cells are the most important part of the body's defense system. The most numerous white blood cells are neutrophils. Their job is to attack and destroy disease-carrying bacteria that enter the body. They do this by surrounding them. Once the bacteria are engulfed, granules inside the cell make chemicals that destroy the invaders and prevent them from multiplying. Neutrophils make up about 60 percent of the white blood cells in the bloodstream.

Eosinophils, which make up about 5 percent of the white blood cells, have three jobs. They help fight bacteria, control the chemical histamine released in the fight, and remove the remains of destroyed cells.

Basophils, which make up about 1 percent of the white blood cells, release a substance that helps prevent blood from always clotting inside the blood vessels.

Lymphocytes, which make up 20 to 30 percent of the white blood cells, participate in the making of antibodies, which are proteins that help the body fight disease.

Monocytes, which make up 5 to 10 percent of the white blood cells, engulf bacteria.

The human body regulates the number of blood cells it makes, according to its needs. If you lose blood, your body produces replacement cells. And when you have an infection, your body makes large numbers of white blood cells to fight it.

The different types ▶ of white blood cells fight against germs.

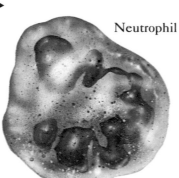
Neutrophil

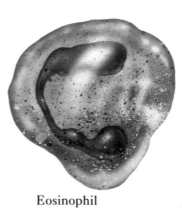
Eosinophil

Basophil

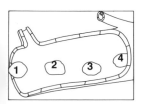

White blood cells move in plasma with the aid of little projections, called pseudopods. When a germ enters the blood, a neutrophil approaches (1), captures (2), and engulfs (3) it, absorbing the germ into the cell before digesting it. (4).

▼

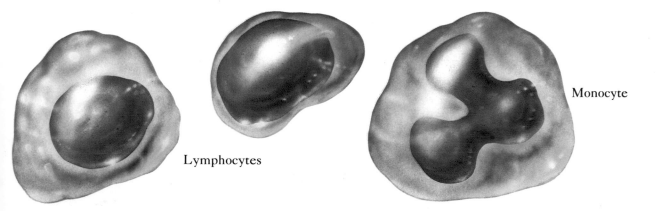

Lymphocytes

Monocyte

Clotting

Clotting is a complicated process that stops the body from losing blood when it is cut from outside, or when blood vessels within the body have been damaged.

Stages in clotting include the tightening of the walls of the cut vessel (vasoconstriction); the releasing of substances that attract platelets to the wounded area; and the production of fibrin, a clot-forming material in the blood.

If the blood vessel is thin, the tightening of the walls will be enough to close off the wound. But when a medium-sized blood vessel is damaged, more help is needed. Large numbers of platelets gather at the wound and stick to the walls of the blood vessels. They form a mass that blocks up the cut.

If the cut is large, the platelets send out chemical messengers that work with other substances in the plasma to make fibrin. A mesh forms across the wound; platelets and red blood cells are trapped in the net; and they form a plug, or scab, that prevents the blood from flowing out and stops infections from getting in while the cell walls repair themselves.

When large blood vessels are cut, the body may not be able to repair itself. Then the edges of the wound must be clamped or sewn together, so that the gap is small enough for the platelets and fibrin to work efficiently.

Some people do not have enough clotting factors in their blood, which means that even a small cut will continue to bleed. These people have the disease hemophilia.

When platelets stick to the walls of a wound, they activate substances in the plasma that form fibrin. This makes a mesh across the wound, which traps parts of the blood and prevents the blood from escaping.

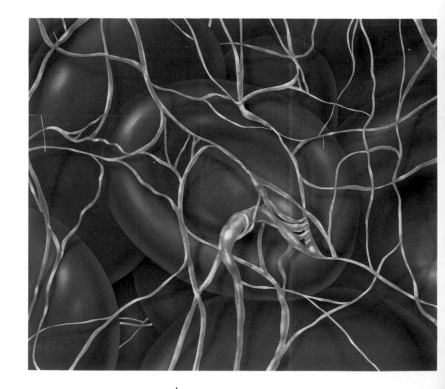

▲
A net of fibrin forms a trap for red blood cells.

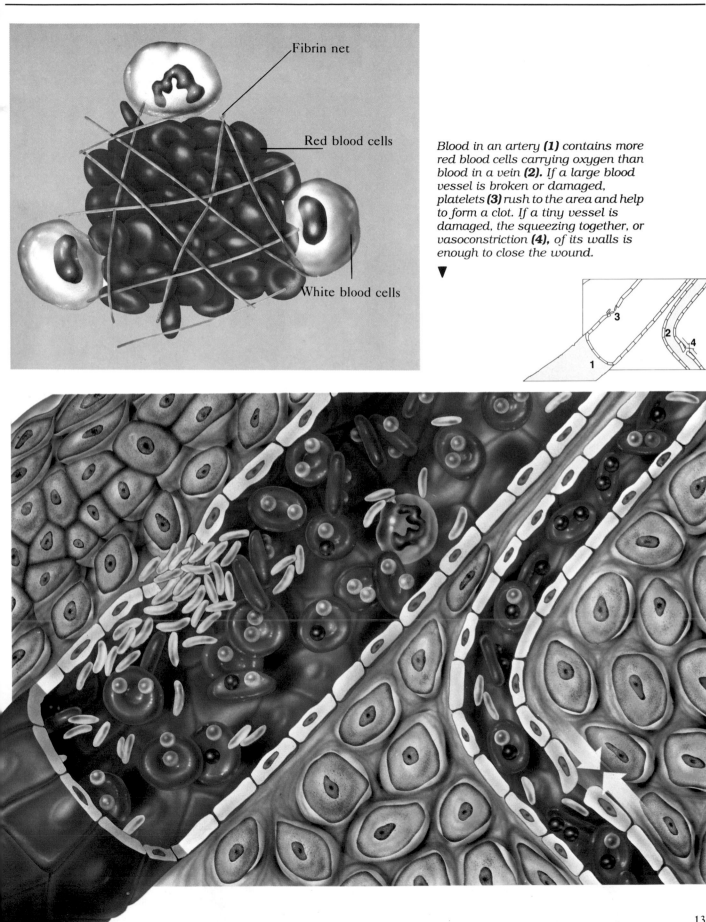

Fibrin net

Red blood cells

White blood cells

Blood in an artery **(1)** contains more red blood cells carrying oxygen than blood in a vein **(2)**. If a large blood vessel is broken or damaged, platelets **(3)** rush to the area and help to form a clot. If a tiny vessel is damaged, the squeezing together, or vasoconstriction **(4)**, of its walls is enough to close the wound.

▼

The Heart

The heart controls the circulation of the blood. It is a muscular organ, about the size of an adult's fist. It has four chambers and is divided down the center by a thick wall of muscle called the septum.

The right side of the heart pumps blood into the lungs. The left side, which is more muscular, pumps blood throughout the body. It takes about 20 seconds for blood to reach every cell in the body.

Each side of the heart is divided into two chambers: the upper chamber (auricle, or atrium) and the lower chamber (ventricle).

The auricles are the heart's receiving chambers, and the ventricles are the heart's pumping chambers. The right atrium is connected to the right ventricle by the tricuspid valve. The left atrium is connected to the left ventricle by the bicuspid, or mitral, valve.

All blood vessels carrying blood out of the heart are called arteries, and all vessels carrying blood back to the heart are known as veins. Arteries have thicker and more muscular walls than veins because they have to withstand higher pressure.

An adult heart is about the size of an adult's fist and weighs between 10 and 13 ounces (300 and 350 grams).

▼

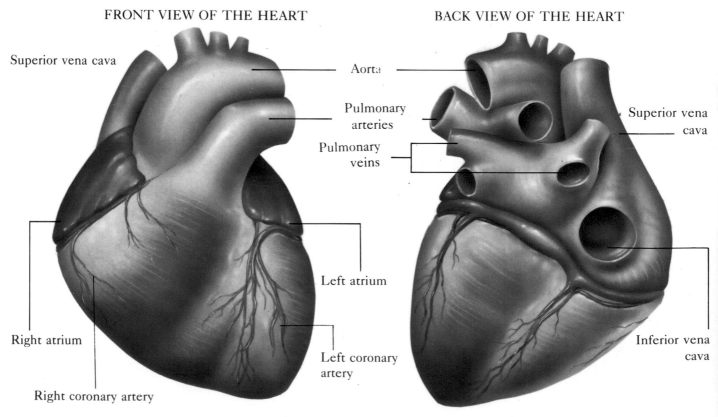

FRONT VIEW OF THE HEART

BACK VIEW OF THE HEART

Superior vena cava

Aorta

Pulmonary arteries

Pulmonary veins

Superior vena cava

Left atrium

Right atrium

Left coronary artery

Right coronary artery

Inferior vena cava

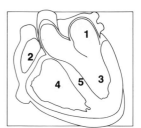

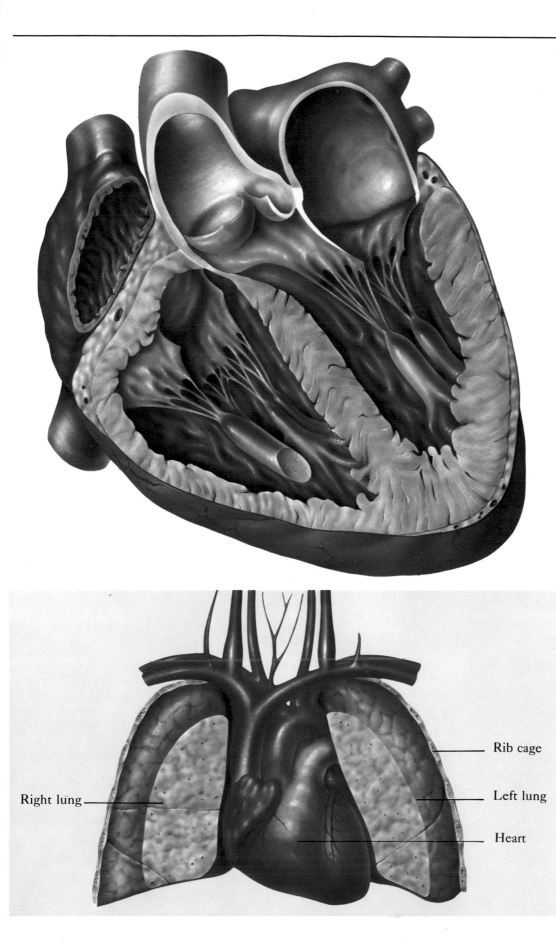

◀ The heart has four chambers: the left atrium **(1)**, the right atrium **(2)**, the left ventricle **(3)**, and the right ventricle **(4)**. The central partition, or septum **(5)**, stops blood in the left side from mixing with blood in the right side.

◀ The heart is positioned between the lungs and slightly to the left in the chest. The ribs arch over to form a protective cage.

Rib cage

Right lung

Left lung

Heart

How the Heart Beats

Your heart beats without stopping throughout your life. It must pump about 2,000 gallons (7,570 liters) of blood daily. To do this, the heart beats, or contracts and relaxes, an average of about 70 times per minute.

When the heart beats, the muscles at the top of the heart contract first. During contractions, the chambers of the heart shorten and harden, just as they lengthen and enlarge during the times of relaxation.

With each contraction, blood is pumped in squirts from the heart's upper chambers to its lower chambers and from the lower chambers into large blood vessels. In between beats, each atrium fills up with blood that will be pumped out with the next heartbeat.

The normal, rhythmic contraction of the heart, or systole, is followed by the closing of the bicuspid and tricuspid valves. The heart's relaxation, or diastole, is followed by the shutting of the valves that lead to the blood vessels.

The regular beating of the heart causes a wave of pressure that forces blood through the arteries. This is known as a pulse. You can feel your pulse by placing your finger against the skin on the inner side of your wrist, just above an artery.

The heart's walls are made of extra-strong muscle called myocardium. This muscle has a lining of thin tissue, the endocardium.

The heart is surrounded by a membrane, pericardium. The space between the pericardium and the heart is filled with pericardial fluid, which cushions and protects the heart and prevents its outer surface from rubbing against other tissues as it beats.

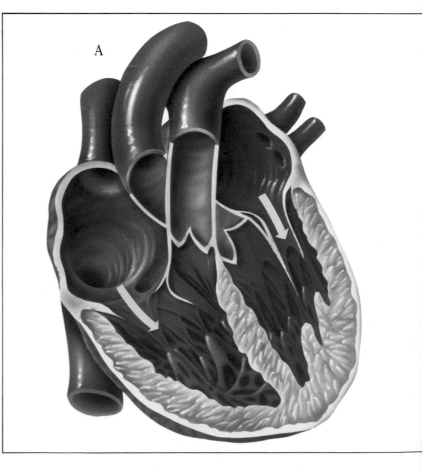

A

The two chambers ▶ in each half of the heart are separated by valves, which have flaps that allow blood to flow in one direction only. The tricuspid valve, which connects the right atrium with the right ventricle, is shown here, open and closed.

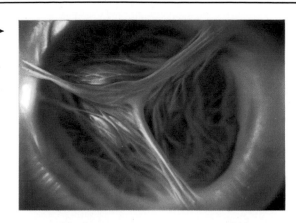

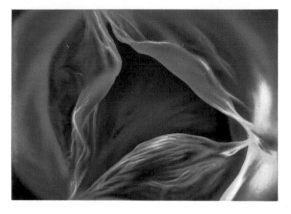

In diagram A, blood in the right atrium (1) flows into the right ventricle (2), and blood in the left atrium (3) flows into the left ventricle (4). In diagram B, the tricuspid valve (1) and mitral valve (2) are closed, so the blood cannot flow back. The pulmonary valve (3) and aortic valve (4) open to let blood through. In diagram C, all the valves (1, 2, 3, and 4) are closed; the heart is in diastole.

▼

B   C

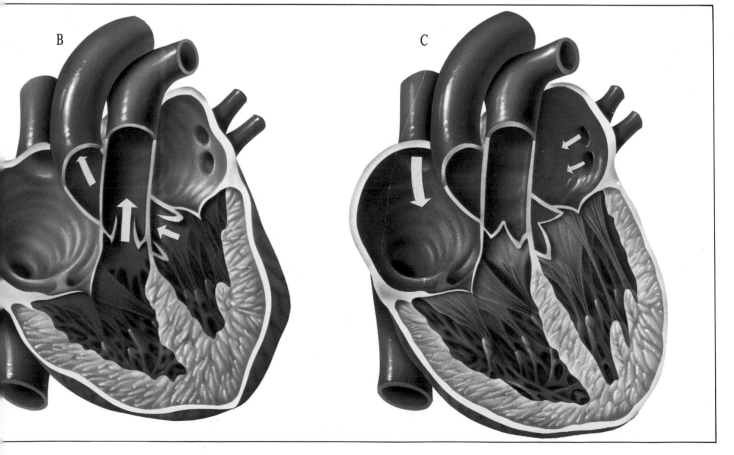

Circulating Oxygen

Blood circulates through the body in two main routes. Systemic circulation carries blood from the heart through the arteries and to all parts of the body except the lungs. After the blood returns to the heart, pulmonary circulation carries it to the lungs, then back to the heart and the systemic route.

In pulmonary circulation, blood containing carbon dioxide leaves the heart by way of the pulmonary artery, which leaves the right ventricle and branches in two. The right branch goes to the right lung and the left branch to the left lung.

In the lungs, each branch divides and subdivides into vessels that become smaller and smaller—the capillary network. Blood flows very quickly through arteries and veins but slowly through capillaries, which allows time for substances to be exchanged through the capillary walls.

The lung tissue contains bunches of tiny, hollow chambers called alveoli, which are surrounded by capillaries. Carbon dioxide from the blood passes through the capillary walls and through the membrane surrounding the alveoli. The carbon dioxide is then breathed out of the lungs.

Oxygen that has been breathed into the lungs moves from the alveoli into the capillaries, where it locks onto hemoglobin molecules in the red

blood cells. These capillaries merge into the right and left lung veins, which take the blood, now rich in oxygen and bright red in color, to the left atrium of the heart.

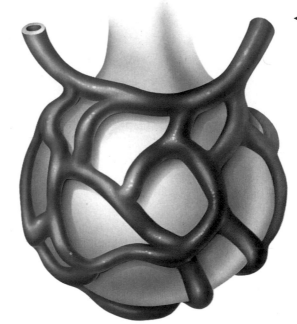

◀ *Air breathed into the lungs is carried into little sacs called alveoli. Their walls are surrounded by a network of capillaries.*

Alveoli are clustered like grapes.

▼

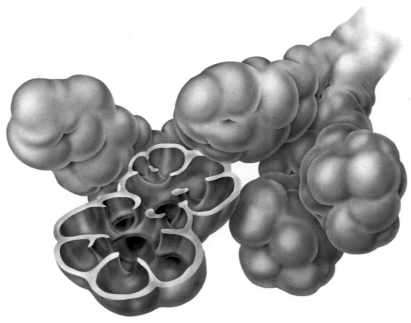

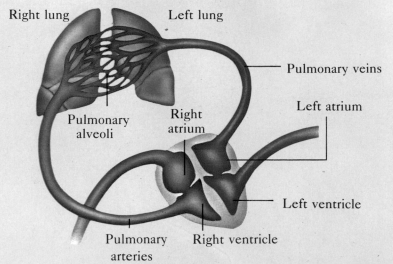

Right lung

Left lung

Pulmonary veins

Pulmonary alveoli

Right atrium

Left atrium

Left ventricle

Pulmonary arteries

Right ventricle

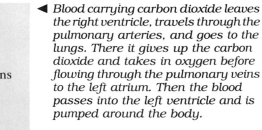

◀ Blood carrying carbon dioxide leaves the right ventricle, travels through the pulmonary arteries, and goes to the lungs. There it gives up the carbon dioxide and takes in oxygen before flowing through the pulmonary veins to the left atrium. Then the blood passes into the left ventricle and is pumped around the body.

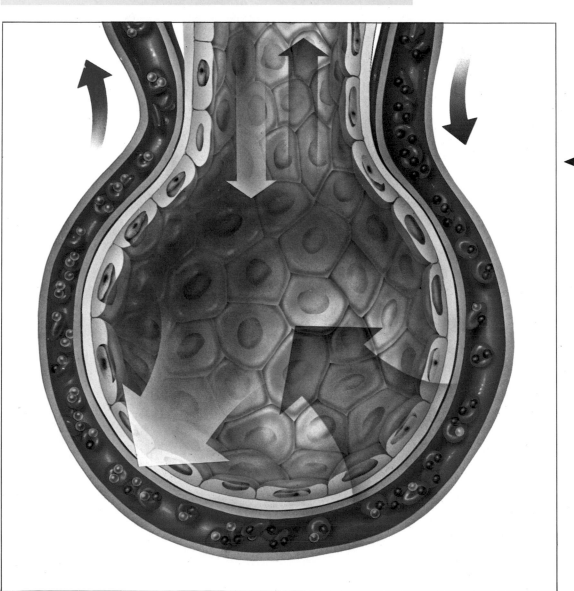

◀ Blood containing carbon dioxide (1) reaches the alveoli. The carbon dioxide (2) passes out through the thin walls of the capillaries into the alveoli and is breathed out of the body. Oxygen (3) passes the opposite way and travels through capillaries that form larger vessels and eventually the pulmonary veins, which take the oxygenated blood (4) to the heart.

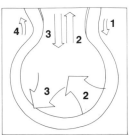

Systemic Circulation

Systemic circulation, which delivers blood to and from all parts of the body, begins in the heart's left ventricle. A contraction of the left ventricle pumps the blood into the aorta, which branches into other arteries.

Once in the arteries, the blood makes its way to smaller arteries and arterioles—and then to the capillaries that border on every cell of the body. There the blood delivers oxygen and nutrients and picks up waste products.

The blood travels back through the capillaries into venules. It then travels through larger and larger veins until it reaches the vena cava. Blood from the head and arms returns to the heart through the superior vena cava, while the inferior vena cava brings blood from the lower parts of the body.

Blood containing oxygen leaves the heart by the aorta and travels through the body. Blood also carries nutrients and waste products on its journey around the body.

▼

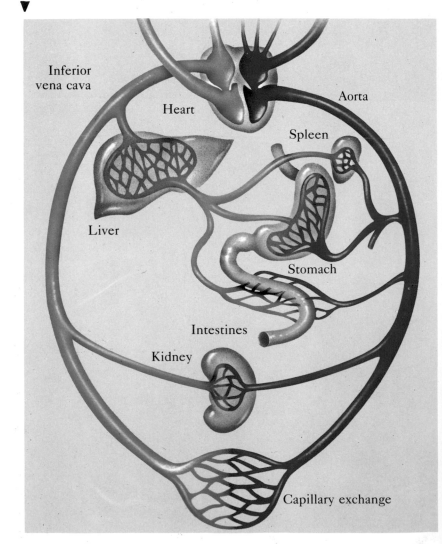

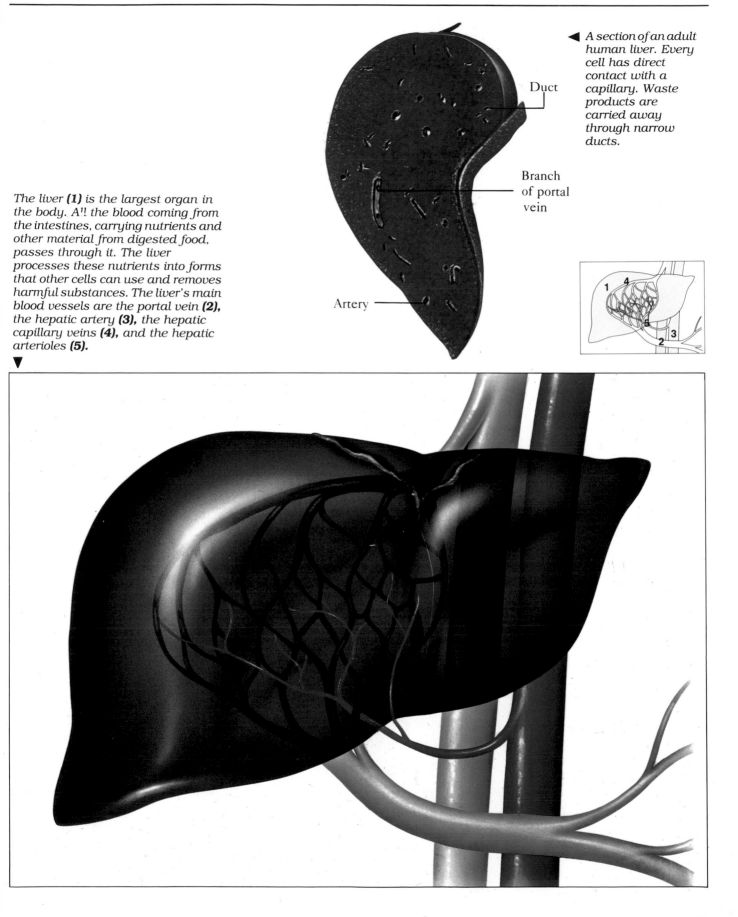

◀ *A section of an adult human liver. Every cell has direct contact with a capillary. Waste products are carried away through narrow ducts.*

Duct

Branch of portal vein

Artery

The liver (1) is the largest organ in the body. A'l! the blood coming from the intestines, carrying nutrients and other material from digested food, passes through it. The liver processes these nutrients into forms that other cells can use and removes harmful substances. The liver's main blood vessels are the portal vein (2), the hepatic artery (3), the hepatic capillary veins (4), and the hepatic arterioles (5).

▼

Blood Vessels

There are more than 60,000 miles (nearly 100,000 kilometers) of blood vessels in an adult's body. All three types of vessels—arteries, veins, and capillaries—are basically hollow tubes, but their structures are not the same.

Arteries carry blood away from the heart. Artery walls are made of strong and elastic tissue, which enables the blood to be pumped under pressure.

Veins carry the blood back to the heart. Their walls are thinner and less elastic than those of the arteries. Valves in the veins prevent blood from flowing in the wrong direction.

There are more capillaries in the body than any other type of blood vessel.

If all of the body's capillaries were laid end to end, they could encircle the equator twice. The walls of capillaries are made up of a single layer of cells, which allows substances to pass through them. The network of capillaries connects the arteries with the veins by linking arterioles and venules.

The circulatory system is a closed-circuit system, although some of the blood's plasma leaves the circuit to form tissue fluid. This fluid bathes the cells of our organs as well as our muscles, fats, and other tissues. It acts as the "go-between" for the blood, enabling it to exchange waste products for nutrients and oxygen.

Blood vessels are the tubes through which the blood circulates. There are three types: arteries, veins, and capillaries. The walls of arteries have three layers. The outer layer is elastic tissue, the middle is muscle, and the inner layer is thin cells that form a smooth lining. Capillaries are very tiny, and their walls are formed from only a single layer of cells.

▼

ARTERY

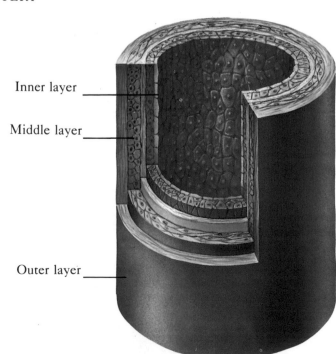

Inner layer

Middle layer

Outer layer

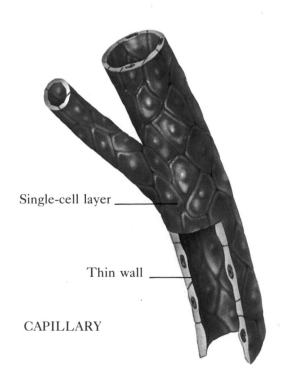

Single-cell layer

Thin wall

CAPILLARY

VEIN

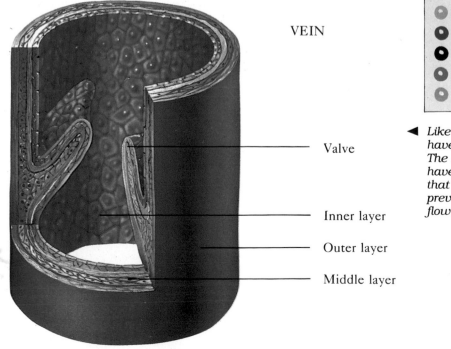

◉	Chlorine
◉	Potassium
◉	Carbon dioxide
◉	Sodium
◉	Oxygen

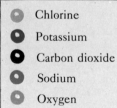

▲ *Chlorine, potassium, carbon dioxide, sodium, and oxygen are constantly being exchanged between the plasma and the tissue fluid.*

◄ *Like arteries, veins have three layers. The larger veins have folds in them that act as valves to prevent blood from flowing back.*

Valve

Inner layer

Outer layer

Middle layer

The Lymph System

Blood is not the only liquid that circulates in our body. The lymph system is also a circulatory system, and it carries the watery fluid called lymph that plays an important part in the body's defense system.

The lymph system collects tissue fluid that has passed from the capillaries to the tissues and takes it back to the veins through two ducts in the neck. The lymph system is made up of a network of capillaries that have closed ends, like the fingers of a glove. They join up with larger vessels, and the lymph is moved around the body by muscle contractions.

Lymph vessels have valves inside, so that the lymph flows only in one direction. They have very fine walls through which proteins and molecules that are too large to be absorbed by the blood capillaries can pass.

The lymph vessels pass through oval-shaped nodules called lymph glands. There are about a hundred lymph glands in the body, mostly in the groin, armpits, and neck. They produce white blood cells (lymphocytes) and antibodies, which fight off infections. Lymph glands also stop infections from spreading through the body by trapping microbes and destroying them.

Lymphatic capillaries are made of very fine tissue, closed at one end but with many pores through which molecules can pass. ▶

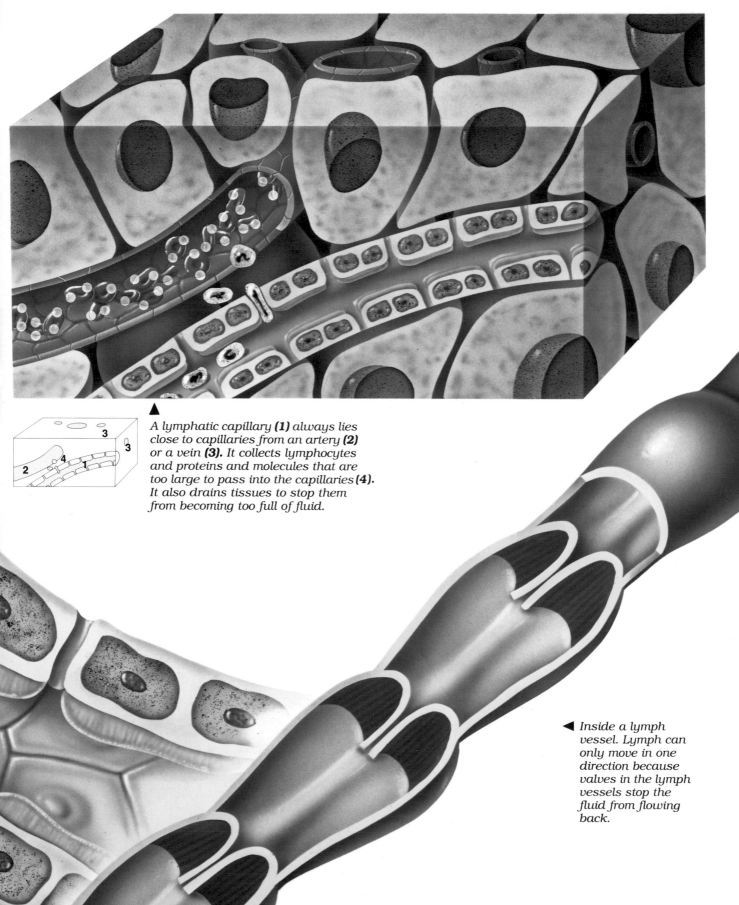

A lymphatic capillary **(1)** always lies close to capillaries from an artery **(2)** or a vein **(3)**. It collects lymphocytes and proteins and molecules that are too large to pass into the capillaries **(4).** It also drains tissues to stop them from becoming too full of fluid.

◀ Inside a lymph vessel. Lymph can only move in one direction because valves in the lymph vessels stop the fluid from flowing back.

Lymph Vessels

The exchange of substances across cell walls is possible because there are differences in pressure between the blood flowing through the veins, the plasma that forms the tissue fluid, and the fluid in the lymph vessels. Fluid always move from higher-pressure areas to lower-pressure areas, keeping a balance between body tissues.

When a person's leg swells, for example, it may be because there is too much fluid in the tissues. The lymph vessels will collect the excess plasma and take it to the veins through the lymph system.

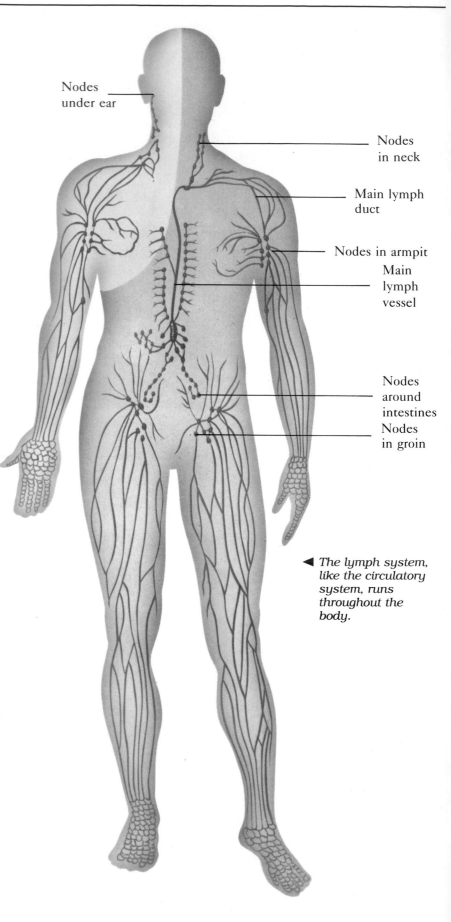

Nodes under ear

Nodes in neck

Main lymph duct

Nodes in armpit

Main lymph vessel

Nodes around intestines

Nodes in groin

◄ The lymph system, like the circulatory system, runs throughout the body.

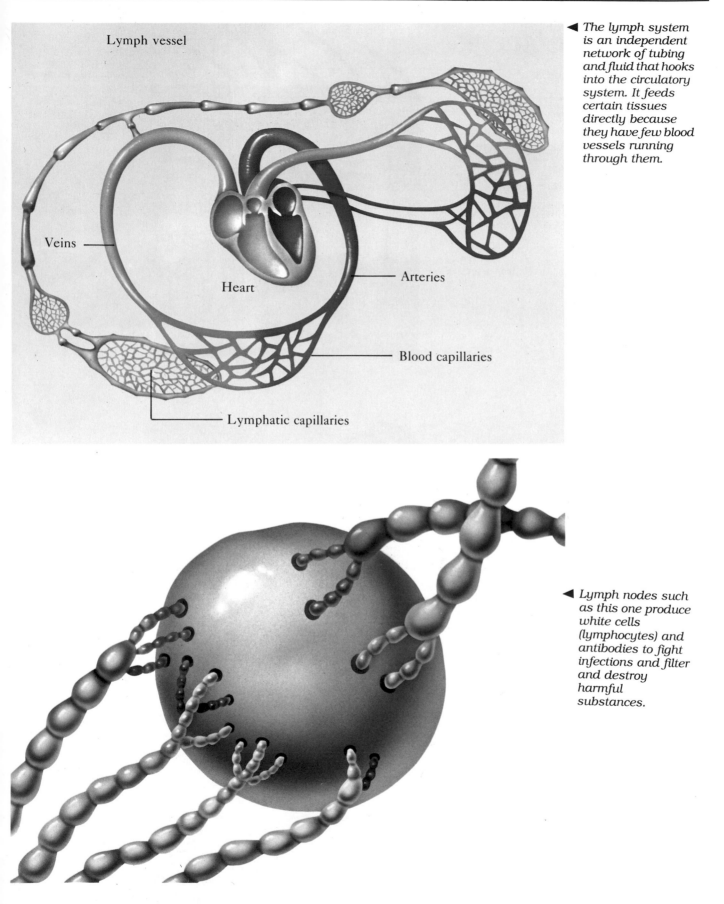

Lymph vessel

Veins

Heart

Arteries

Blood capillaries

Lymphatic capillaries

◀ *The lymph system is an independent network of tubing and fluid that hooks into the circulatory system. It feeds certain tissues directly because they have few blood vessels running through them.*

◀ *Lymph nodes such as this one produce white cells (lymphocytes) and antibodies to fight infections and filter and destroy harmful substances.*

27

Simple Experiments

Temperature Control

Blood is a good conductor of heat, and it plays an important part in keeping our body temperature steady. When we are hot, capillaries just beneath the skin grow wider to allow more blood to go to the body's surface, and some of our body heat escapes into the air.

When we are cold, the capillaries grow thinner, and less blood goes to the skin. This means that less heat is lost.

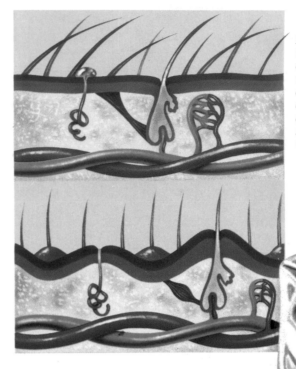

Press your finger lightly on an ice cube. Your fingertip will turn pale as the capillaries constrict and force blood away from the surface.
▼

Taking Your Pulse

To take your pulse, hold your hand and press lightly with your first three fingers on the large artery that flows on the thumb side of your wrist. You should be able to feel a steady throbbing. This pulse is the wave action of blood through your arteries, set up by the beating of your heart.

◄ *To take your pulse, hold your wrist and place your middle finger on an artery, counting the number of throbs in a minute.*

Working Harder

When you exercise, your cells work harder than normal, and so they need extra fuel. This means that the blood needs to travel faster around the body to supply them, and so your heart needs to beat faster. The heart of an adult at rest normally beats about 70 times a minute. Exercise can increase the total to well over 100 beats a minute.

Blood Groups

There are four blood groups—A, B, AB, and O—and two types of antigens: A and B. When someone loses a lot of blood, they may need to be given blood from another person. It is vital that this blood should be compatible with the person's own blood group. Also, if a person is given blood containing the wrong type of antigens, antibodies will attack it.

Take your pulse while you are at rest. Then do some push-ups. You will find that exercise causes the pulse rate to increase sharply.
▼

▼ This blood transfusion chart shows the antigens (A or B) and antibodies (anti-A and anti-B) each group contains, and who can give and receive blood among the four groups.

BLOOD GROUP	ANTIGEN	ANTIBODY	CAN GIVE BLOOD TO	CAN RECEIVE BLOOD FROM	WHO HAS THIS GROUP?
O	Neither	Anti-A and Anti-B	Anyone	O	Most Common
A	A	Anti-B	A and AB	A and O	Common
B	B	Anti-A	B and AB	B and O	Rare
AB	A and B	Neither	AB	Anybody	Rarest

Glossary

alveoli *tiny air-filled sacs in the lungs, from which blood takes up oxygen*

antibody *a protein produced by the body to fight bacteria, viruses, and other foreign substances*

antigen *a substance that stimulates the production of antibodies*

aorta *the largest artery in the body*

arteriole *a small artery*

artery *a blood vessel that carries blood away from the heart*

atrium *the two upper chambers of the heart*

auricle *an atrium*

basophil *a type of white blood cell*

bicuspid valve *a valve with two flaps between the left ventricle and left atrium of the heart*

blood group *one of four groups into which blood is classified, depending on which antigens it contains*

bone marrow *soft tissue found in some bones*

capillary *a microscopic, connecting blood vessel*

clot *a thick, jellylike mass produced by platelets*

corpuscle *any cell or small mass not connected to form continuous tissue*

diastole *the phase in the heart's beating cycle in which its ventricles are relaxed*

endocardium *the thin layer of tissue that lines the heart*

eosinophil *a type of white blood cell*

erythrocyte *a red blood cell*

fibrin *a fibrous, clot-forming material in the blood*

hemoglobin *an iron compound in red blood cells that carries oxygen from the lungs to the body's tissues*

hemophilia *a hereditary disease characterized by a lack of blood clotting factors*

heparin *a substance that helps prevent blood from clotting*

leucocyte *a white blood cell*

lymph system *an independent circulation system that carries lymph and waste products around the body*

monocyte *a type of white blood cell*

myocardium *the muscular tissue that forms the walls of the heart*

neutrophil *a type of white blood cell*

pericardium *the sac surrounding and covering the heart*

plasma *the liquid part of blood*

platelet *blood cells that control clotting*

pulmonary circulation *the route of blood to and from the lungs*

pulse *the regular wave of pressure through the arteries, caused by the beating of the heart*

systemic circulation *the route of blood to and from body parts*

systole *the phase in the heart's beating cycle in which the muscles are contracted*

tricuspid valve *a valve with three flaps that separates the right ventricle and right atrium of the heart*

vasoconstriction *the tightening of capillary walls to narrow the blood vessels*

vein *a blood vessel that carries blood from the body back to the heart*

vena cava *the two large veins that return blood to the right atrium of the heart*

ventricle *the two lower chambers of the heart*

venule *a small vein*

Index

Alveoli, 18, 19
Amino acids, 8
Antibody, 6, 24, 29
Antigen, 29
Aorta, 14, 17, 20
Arteriole, 4, 20, 21
Artery, 4, 5, 13, 14, 16, 18–22, 26, 27
Atrium, 14–17, 20
Auricle, 14

Bacteria, 10
Basophil, 10
Bicuspid valve, 14, 16, 17
Blood group, 29
Bone marrow, 6, 8, 9

Capillary, 4, 5, 18–22, 24–28
Carbon dioxide, 8, 14, 18, 19, 20, 22, 23
Clotting, 5, 6, 10, 12, 13
Corpuscle, 6

Defense system, 5, 6, 10, 24, 25
Diastole, 16, 17
Digestive system, 8
Duct, 26, 27

Endocardium, 16
Eosinophil, 10
Erythrocyte, 6

Fibrin, 12, 13

Globin, 8

Heart, 4, 14–20, 27
Heme molecules, 8
Hemoglobin, 6, 18
Hemophilia, 12
Heparin, 12
Histamine, 10
Hormone, 4, 6, 20

Kidney, 4, 20

Leucocyte, 6
Liver, 4, 20, 21
Lung, 4, 14, 15, 18, 19, 20
Lymph, 24, 27
Lymphocytes, 6, 10, 11, 24, 27
Lymph system, 24, 27

Microbe, 6, 24
Minerals, 6, 20
Monocyte, 6, 11
Myocardium, 16

Neutrophil, 10, 11
Nutrient, 4, 20–22

Oxygen, 4–6, 8, 13, 14, 18–20, 22, 23

Pericardium, 16
Plasma, 6, 11, 12, 22, 23, 26
Platelet, 5–7, 9, 12, 13
Pulmonary artery, 14, 17–19
Pulmonary circulation, 18, 19
Pulmonary vein, 14
Pulse, 16, 28, 29

Red blood cells, 5–9, 12, 13

Spleen, 4, 8, 20
Systemic circulation, 18, 20, 21
Systole, 16

Thrombocyte, 6
Thyroid gland, 4
Tricuspid valve, 14, 16, 17

Vasoconstriction, 12, 13
Vein, 4, 13, 16, 18–27
Vena cava, 14, 20
Ventricle, 14–20
Venule, 20

White blood cells, 5–7, 9–13, 24, 26, 27